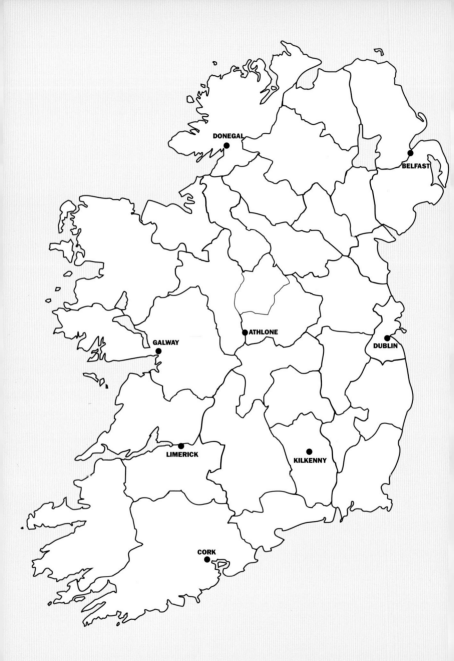

The Magic of
Ireland

ROB VANCE photographs and writes about Ireland with a special focus on its history, identity and beliefs. He has written and presented several series for RTÉ television, including 'The Island', 'Secret Sights' and 'Urban Tales'. This is his fifth book.

ACKNOWLEDGEMENTS

With thanks to Jocelyn Vance and Kevin McGilligan for their photographic assistance, and to Claudia Köhler of the Medieval Education Centre for reading the text and for her encouragement. Special thanks to the staff of The O'Brien Press, especially Helen Carr and Emma Byrne.

THE MAGIC OF
Ireland

ROB VANCE

THE O'BRIEN PRESS
DUBLIN

First published 2007 by the O'Brien Press Ltd,
12 Terenure Road East, Rathgar, Dublin 6, Ireland.
Tel: +353 1 4923333; Fax: +353 1 4922777
E-mail: books@obrien.ie
Website: www.obrien.ie

ISBN: 978-1-84717-001-9

British Library Cataloguing in Publication Data
Vance, Robert
The magic of Ireland
1. Ireland - Description and travel
I. Title
914.1'5'04824

1 2 3 4 5 6 7 8 9 10
07 08 09 10 11 12

Printed and bound by KHL, Singapore

CONTENTS

The doorway of Tristernagh Friary, Co. Westmeath, where sixteenth-century tenants of the monks paid a 'porker', two chickens and twenty-six gallons of beer as Christmas rent.

INTRODUCTION

I reland is subtly different to other lands; it has a unique compound of weather, landscape, people, and that something extra – the remnants of a pagan and medieval past. These elements of people and place combine to give the country a certain magic all its own. This magic can be found throughout the country; it can be felt at ancient horse fairs and in the melodies of traditional musicians, it can be seen in ruined castles and in dramatic skies that change by the hour. At holy wells or stone circles it is sometimes possible to catch that spirit of a place, the suggestion that a tiny spark of old events may inhabit a physical place, catching the corner of the eye and tingling the very edge of the senses.

The hills and valleys of Ireland are overlaid with stories from Celtic mythology. These strange, thousand-year-old narratives tell of warrior queens and powerful druids, heroes taking epic journeys to learn the magic arts, or to win a kingdom or a bride. Celts brought many of these tales to Ireland millennia ago and enigmatic place names – like Ardee, 'The Ford of Ferdia', in County Louth, which commemorates a mythical battle – recall their legends.

Evening sun catches the carved head of a stylised Gaelic king on the chancel arch of 12th century Kilteel Church in County Kildare. He may be the benefactor of the church, his face carved in the likeness of King David from the Old Testament.

Modern Irish towns straddle roads that once carried the chariots of kings; many of those ancient route-ways still exist, hidden beneath secondary roads and lanes. These narrow chariot roads sometimes turn suddenly across farmland, their junctions marked by tall standing stones. Many are dotted with intermittent burial mounds, reminders that life in Celtic times was heroic, brutal and often short. The Slighe Mór, the chariot road from Tara to the West of Ireland remembered in sagas and by saints, terminates at the muddy shore beyond Clarinbridge in County Galway where mallards and pintail duck spend mild winters.

Ireland is still a land of spirituality, and pagan and early Christian monuments often overlap; former druids

The Slighe Mór, the ancient chariot route to the west meanders through County Westmeath near the village of Glasson.

exchanged magic for the mass, combining daily prayers with occasional spells to change the weather. Some Irish churches have been in continuous use since their foundation. In County Kildare, St Brigid's well and church have origins in the saint's own time, when she founded a monastery there. There are many ancient holy wells scattered across the country that are still visited by those in need today.

The Vikings, dangerous sea-borne pirates from Scandinavia, first raided Ireland in 795 AD and ultimately founded many towns, like Arklow and Carlingford, together with four Irish cities: Dublin, Cork, Waterford and Limerick. Their skill on the seas allowed them to create communities that traded amber from Russia for Irish slaves to Baghdad. Shortly after settling, these Danes and Norwegians intermarried with the Irish, their descendants becoming MacAuliffe and McIvor instead of Olaf and Ivar. Many of Ireland's city dwellers are the descendants of those intrepid sailors.

The Welsh Normans came to Dublin in 1167; they too left their mark on the city, building the cathedral of the Holy Trinity, now Christchurch Cathedral, on the site of a Viking timber church. These armour-clad knights spread throughout Ireland, ultimately adapting to Irish ways, and like the Vikings, changing, as De Burgo became Burke and De Caunteton, Staunton, while the FitzGeralds of Kildare

The 'Hogback' grave of a Viking warrior in Castledermot churchyard, Co. Kildare.

and Limerick changed from Norman *conquistadors* to Irish-speaking nobility.

A Norman knight, known as Fada *or Tall Cantwell, settled in Kilkenny and left this effigy to himself.*

This island still has more ancient monuments per square hectare than any other country in Europe, and the high crosses and early monasteries testify to its rich cultural life during Europe's Dark Ages when Ireland was known as a land of scholars.

The early medieval period produced a wealth of art and artefact and places of contemplation. The Early Christian period has left stone beehive huts and tiny churches whose claustrophobic darkness seems to envelop the soul. As the middle ages began, gothic cathedrals replaced the romanesque exuberance of native art and gradually the bestiary of the archway gave way to a more restrained and orthodox

form of architecture. Many medieval abbeys and friaries are treasure houses of stone saints, mitred bishops and proud knights, whose limestone features illustrate the sophisticated society that Ireland had become by the middle ages.

Tomb of an unknown Irish chieftain in Kilconnell Friary, County Galway, one of the many Gaelic nobles who endowed churches and were interred within the walls when they died.

In the medieval period, Ireland was a land of many independent principalities where nobles, ladies and chieftains married, fought and made deals with each other, in a similar fashion to medieval Italy. Many ruined churches hold the flamboyant tombs of their founders, an O'Hara, a Burke or an O'Connor;

some seem to echo still to the sound of psalms, centuries after their foundation.

A foliate grave slab in Movilla Abbey, County Down, whose scissors detail designates an Irish noblewoman of the thirteenth century.

Ireland is still primarily agricultural, as it has been for millennia and, outside the towns and cities, the predominant geological underlay of limestone in the central plain ensures sweet and abundant grass for cattle and the important dairy industry.

When you travel around the island, magic may suddenly appear when light creates unexpected colour in a grey landscape, as a burst of sun throws gorse blossom into vibrant relief against skies as black as wet slate.

A bull jealously guards his 'harem' of cows on the lush pastures of County Westmeath.

Even on a calm summer's day, one may see small clouds quickly scudding across a clear sky pursued by some high, Atlantic breeze. Everywhere the light shapes the senses, illuminating recent and distant memories hidden in the landscape. And it can be seasonal, as in March and April, when spring showers seem to travel the country like a carnival, creating rainbows that briefly unite earth and sky. On midland roads, rain-soaked fields carry sleek, black cattle next to luxuriant meadows where yellow rapeseed seems like a virtual crop, coloured by a surrealist.

Ireland is also a place of towns and cities. Urban life has long been established, with Waterford vying with Dublin for the title of oldest settlement. Both were established by Irish and Vikings over a thousand years ago, then walled in stone by Normans, subsequently going through the ups and downs of siege, plague, reformation and rebuilding that turned medieval cities into cosmopolitan centres with

Rathlin Island caught with a rainbow.

theatres, restaurants and fine public buildings.

Brian Boru, who defeated the Vikings of Limerick before attempting to become the High King of Ireland by defeating the Vikings of Dublin. This nineteenth-century bust looks out from the Chapel Royal of Dublin Castle.

Old traditions continue. Now surrounded by modern apartment blocks, the Smithfield Horse Fair has echoes of the early Irish fairs – *'oenach'* – held as far back as the ninth century. At those gatherings, tribal elders settled disputes, held horse races and conducted business. Modern fairs are centred on economic activity, but many have the chaotic exuberance of a pagan gathering, as horses, children, hawkers and hucksters mingle and jostle in the pursuit of a good bargain.

But the magic of Ireland lies also in its people – black-haired, red-haired, blond and brown, with eyes of blue, green, brown and grey. As people after people settled on the island at the edge of the world, they brought with them

Street musicians playing traditional melodies enliven Dublin's streets.

language and music, wit and imagination, combining Celt, Viking, Norman and Elizabethan, to create the Irish of today. Ireland's remote location seemed to trap many ancient traditions as if in amber, and bring them almost intact into the twenty-first century. When you hear Irish music, you hear sounds that were first heard perhaps 1,500 years ago, when pipers and harpists played for the early saints. And the blend still continues today as new waves of people arrive, creating the Ireland and the Irish music of tomorrow.

This book is an introduction to the magic of Ireland and its people.

The entrance to the Otherworld: Knowth Passage Tomb, built over 5,000 years ago by an advanced agrarian society that completely disappeared, leaving only enigmatic mounds and inscriptions.

THE NORTH

The North of Ireland has been known as 'Ulster' since the earliest historic period. The name combines '*Ulaidh*', the name of a tribal grouping based around Armagh, and the Viking word '*ster*', meaning homestead. Over two thousand years ago the Ulaidh constructed a series of earthworks, known to mythology as 'The Black Pig's Dyke', to defend their northern territory; traces of these massive banks still meander across the north midlands, connecting lakes, hills and long-vanished forests. It protected the capital of ancient Ulster, Eamhain Mhaca, a grassy hill named after the horse goddess Mhaca, a goddess of fertility often depicted with a bird on her shoulder. It was the tribal centre where the young warrior Cú Chulainn learnt the

Rampart of the Dorsey, ancient southern gateway through the Black Pig's Dyke lies submerged by two millennia of vegetation.

arts of war from Conor Mac Nessa, a pagan king surrounded by warriors and beautiful women.

Christianity came to Ulster in the fifth century and the village of Carndonagh in County Donegal holds an interesting collection of ancient monuments from that time, comprising an early Christian cross and other stones that are possibly pagan. While the cross itself is eighth-century, the stones nearby pre-date it, being the original objects of pre-Christian veneration. A strange cowled figure glowers at the onlooker from one stone while another has a man with a

headdress that resembles 'Mickey Mouse' ears, similar to those from Celtic regions of Germany.

Up to five hundred years ago Ireland was densely forested and Ulster had some of the largest woods on the island, like The Fews, Killultagh, Killetra, Glenconkeyne – the last covering hundreds of square kilometres and renowned for its deer and wolves. Most of these great forests were cut down after the plantation of Ulster in 1608, when the Gaelic nobility emigrated and their lands were confiscated, cleared of trees and planted with settlers from Scotland. This road near Bailieborough in County Cavan retains its tall and elegant beeches planted in the eighteenth century by an improving landlord.

BELFAST CASTLE, BELFAST, CO. ANTRIM

Belfast Castle, built by the Chichester family to overlook the city they owned, is in a Scottish baronial style and sits beneath brooding Cave Hill, now a National Park. The city of Belfast itself is predominantly Victorian, many of its buildings dating from the industrial boom of the nineteenth century when shipbuilding, engineering, rope works and linen made it Ireland's industrial heartland. It still retains a somewhat gruff air of business and no-nonsense. Its people are friendly, its parks well-kept and

planted, and its city hall, built
in the late nineteenth century,
is a fine example of Victorian
architecture.

THE GLENS OF ANTRIM, CO. ANTRIM

The Glens of Antrim have
retained their own identity, a mixture of Gael and Scot, and
have their own distinct culture and history. The dialect of
Irish common to the Glens is very similar to that spoken
on the Scottish coast less than twenty miles away and the
inhabitants shared cross-channel musical and farming

practices well into the twentieth century. The meandering roads and gentle inclines of the Glens are sometimes illuminated by brilliant sunshine and spectacular rainbows during the spring months.

THE SPANISH ARMADA

In 1588 a great armada of over 120 galleons sailed to attack England and force it back to Catholicism. It was defeated and the vast fleet was scattered in a violent storm off Donegal. The galleon *Girona* had over 1,500 souls on board, the survivors of several Armada wrecks, when it split apart at Lacada Point where an inlet now called *Port na Spainigh* (The Port of the Spanish) meets the sea. Only a handful survived. The location of the wreck remained a

Gold doubloons and 'Pieces-of-Eight' from the Girona, a Galleass that foundered on the Ulster coast in 1588 after the defeat of the Spanish Armada.

mystery until 1967 when Robert Stenuit, a Belgian marine archaeologist located the remains.

The Ulster Museum in Belfast now has the largest collection of artefacts and cannon from this era, salvaged from several of the twenty-five or more galleons that foundered along the Irish coasts.

A 'Morion', worn by Spanish infantrymen in the 16th century and recovered from an Armada wreck.

CLONES CROSS, CLONES, CO. MONAGHAN

St Tighernach founded a monastery in Clones and the Round Tower survives. He came here in the sixth century and the cross dates from some centuries later. It was moved to the centre of what was a thriving market town and may originally have been two separate crosses joined together, as it incorporates two different styles. The lower part of the cross shows the Fall of Man, while the head is subtly different in execution.

DONEGAL CASTLE, CO. DONEGAL

Donegal Castle, in Donegal town, was the home of Ineen Dubh O'Donnell, one of the most formidable women of sixteenth-century Irish politics who combined a subtle intellect with courage and beauty. She was a Scot, the daughter of a MacDonald of the Isles and instead of the usual wedding dowry of money or household goods she brought a small army of Redshanks – Scottish mercenary soldiers who made sure their mistress was obeyed and respected. Following the 1608 departure of the Northern Gaelic nobility, including her son, and the confiscation of their land, she remained in Ulster, farming a reduced estate as an independent and proud landowner in her own right.

GLENCOLMCILLE, CO. DONEGAL

When Fr James McDyer, a resolute and imaginative priest, arrived in the remote valley of Glencolmcille in 1951 the area was ravaged by unemployment and emigration. He dedicated himself to promoting the local culture, encouraging tourism and setting up agricultural and knitting collectives. Thanks to his efforts, and those of the local people, the village is thriving and their Folk Village Museum and Heritage Centre can still be visited today. There are many dolmens in the area, and a pillar cross dating from the early Christian era at which prayers are still said.

THE CLIFFS OF SLIEVE LEAGUE, CO. DONEGAL

Coloured ochre by the evening sun, the highest sea-cliffs in Europe rise almost six hundred metres above the Atlantic. They echo to the cries of thousands of herring gulls whose keen eyes watch the boats returning to

Killybegs, the northern home of the Irish fishing fleet. These high cliffs have a mesmeric quality, pulling the unwary toward a precarious and risky walk along the rim. But sudden strong gusts can disorientate even a sturdy climber and several have had to be rescued by helicopter. Others have not been so lucky.

BEAGHMORE, CO. TYRONE

This extraordinary site was completely forgotten and lost until quite recently. It was created almost four thousand years ago, perhaps as an observatory and ritual site for the people who farmed the high pastures of the Sperrin Mountains. As the climate gradually got colder, they may

have built more and more elaborate stone alignments to try to entice the sun god to return. The peat grew in the now colder climate until it covered the site to a depth of two metres and it was only in the 1940s that turf cutters gradually unearthed dozens of monoliths. There may be several more rows of stones under the surrounding uncut bog. Even today this remote site retains a sense of these farmers of old, trying desperately to recall their sun god, hoping he would warm the chill that gradually enveloped and annihilated their community.

LURIGETHAN, CO. ANTRIM

The mountain of Lurigethan was fortress and farm to Celtic settlers and traders who came to this area around two thousand years ago. They may have been Venetii, a tribal group who favoured coastal peninsulas, digging deep ditches across the narrow access point to prevent attack. The coasts of Ireland have many such peninsula forts, especially along the south and east coasts. These traders may have settled in Ireland following their defeat in Gaul (modern France) by Caesar in 55 BC. This mountain fortress has similar ditches and is a sort of mountain peninsula, from where the Venetii could observe the coast.

GIANTS' CAUSEWAY, CO. ANTRIM

Strange basalt columns, the result of molten volcanic

rock meeting freezing sea, project from the coast in Antrim, suggesting the mysterious causeway of Fionn MacCumhaill, a giant of the legendary past. Hundreds of these columns form what seem to be the foundations of a truly giant project, giving the impression of a mighty builder abandoning the site, never to return. Hexagons and pentagons form terraces and platforms of continuous regularity and preciseness, and it's easy to understand how the causeway was long understood to have been the work of some extraordinary power. The causeway only became a tourist attraction after 1837 when the coast road was built between Larne and Portrush and it soon became one of Ulster's main tourist attractions. It is now a geological Wonder of the World and has an interpretive centre and a coffee shop.

DUNLUCE, CO. ANTRIM

The castle of Dunluce was built in the fourteenth century on a site fortified by Vikings centuries earlier. It was a seat of Richard de Burgh, Earl of Ulster, but was eventually taken by the warlike MacDonnell family whose territory included land in Scotland. They were involved in Irish and Scottish politics and succeeded in backing more winners than losers in the turbulent middle ages. They resisted English domination for centuries and were one of

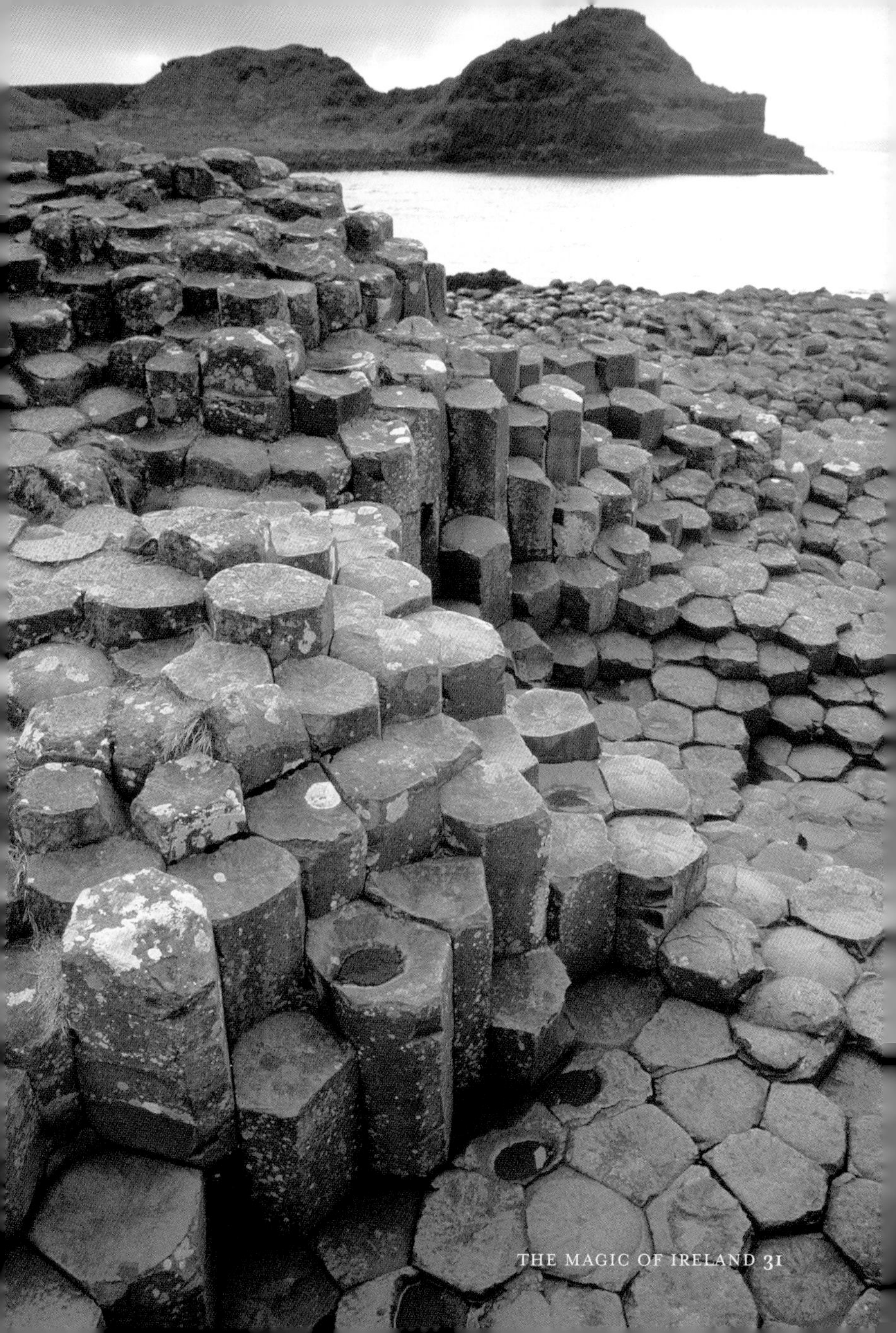

the few families to help survivors of the Spanish Armada of 1588. The castle was abandoned by the MacDonnells shortly after the wing containing the kitchens and staff fell into the sea during a raging storm in 1639.

LOUGH ERNE, CO. FERMANAGH

Lough Erne covers several hundred square miles and offers boating, sailing and fishing from villages around its shores.

The town of Enniskillen is a major centre for the region and has a waterbus service taking tourists from island to island during the summer. This beautiful lake is home to colonies of geese, swans and otters.

A red postbox on the shores of Lough Erne.

THE WEST

The West

The west of Ireland broadly covers the ancient province of Connacht and has its own unique cultural identity and linguistic lilt. It has the highest number of Irish speakers in the country, the national Irish-language radio and TV stations are based there, and its arts and film festivals attract the very best of international talent. The landscape of Connemara with its mountains, bogs and Atlantic beaches offers an unrivalled natural diversity and has proved popular with tourists, painters and filmmakers. Well into the twentieth century it was considered a remote, wild place. It has retained a special place in the Irish imagination, a sort of dream homeland, a nirvana perhaps, dramatised by JM Synge and others who revealed a passionate and eloquent society beneath the poverty and apparent rural simplicity.

This standing stone is one of a series of monoliths that

lie between Croagh Patrick, Ireland's holy mountain, and the sea. The mountain itself was a holy place before Christianity, a mystical peak where the gods were believed to live. Every July to this day thousands make the pilgrimage up the 'Reek' of Saint Patrick, who reputedly banished those gods from their elevated home.

The monoliths are partially submerged in the boggy fields beside the road, encrusted with lichens and moss, and often hidden in mist and sheets of rain. They are, therefore, rarely visited and so can usually be viewed in peace and solitude.

ROSS ERRILY FRIARY, CO. GALWAY

In the fifteenth century, the Franciscans enjoyed huge popularity in east Galway and as their vocations increased, so did their buildings. The friary of Ross Errily was founded by Richard de Burgo and is the most extensive in Ireland. It includes a very large church, with galleries, dormitories, a communal loo (*necessarium*) and a fish tank to give a varied diet. The friary is surrounded by its original

farmland and retains a wonderful atmosphere of tranquillity and peace.

GALWAY CITY, CO. GALWAY

This thriving university and commercial centre of Connacht was a walled city-state in medieval Ireland,

enjoying virtual autonomy and free trade due to its charters, the earliest of which dates to around 1270. It was ruled by an oligarchy of merchant families such as Blake, Bodkin, Joyce, Lynch and Kirwan.

Today's Galway is host to the weekly organic market, which brings producers from across the west of Ireland with vegetables, herbs, cheese and exotic bread. It follows an old tradition of markets in the medieval city and shelters beneath the church of St Nicholas, visited by Christopher Columbus in 1492. The church itself has a fine collection of fifteenth- and sixteenth-century tombs and stone carvings, some damaged by the Cromwellians who used the church as a stable in the 1650s.

Exuberant Victorian department stores are a feature of the streets of Galway, where locally produced woollen goods and the latest digital cameras share window space. The streets and lanes follow the curves of the walled medieval town and shops and pubs often contain low pointed doorways or gothic windows alongside the neon and plate glass. The city is renowned as a centre of music and pub life, called 'craic', where conversation and strong drink can lead to the problems of the world being resolved by the early morning.

CARRIGAHOWLEY, CO. MAYO

Carrigahowley (overleaf) was one of the castles of Grace O'Malley, also known as Granuaile, a formidable pirate of the western seas in the sixteenth century and chieftain of the O'Malleys. She was a competent leader of her people and sailed to London in 1593 to negotiate with Queen Elizabeth I, thereby enabling the O'Malleys to retain a considerable portion of their lands despite the efforts of English adventurers and officials.

MOYNE FRIARY, CO. MAYO

Moyne Friary, County Mayo, was founded in the sixteenth century by a MacWilliam Burke for the Franciscans. The Franciscans were welcomed in the west of Ireland since the sixteenth century and operated an equitable system whereby they recruited their friars from the local people and established an intimate relationship with all social classes. Many of these friaries were built in a piecemeal fashion as funds became available.

THE DOLMEN OF BALLINA, CO. MAYO

The Dolmen of Ballina, perhaps more than four thousand years old, sits on a low hill outside the town. It was probably a ritual site, centred on the cremated burials of its ruling elite, who were most likely kings and also priests.

ENNIS FRIARY, ENNIS, CO. CLARE

This friary was founded before 1250 by the Macnamaras and incorporates pieces of an earlier castle built by Thomas de Clare. It contains many tombs of the Macnamaras who were the dominant Gaelic family of the area. On sunny days when the light dapples through the stone cloister arcades it is reminiscent of Assisi, the Italian monastery of St Francis, founder of the order.

GLENCAR LOUGH, CO. LEITRIM

Glencar Lough in Leitrim is surrounded by escarpments and mountains and offers spectacular pike fishing on its deep waters. Legend has it that the lake is home to the Doberchu, a monster of the lake that was last seen in 1722, when it reputedly savaged a local girl. The cliffs above the lake are home to a variety of Alpine plants such as saxifrage and mountain avens, but perhaps the real charm of the area is its secluded nature, hidden in the Glencar valley west of Sligo that connects the spectacular highlands of County Leitrim to the coast.

STREEDAGH POINT, CO. SLIGO

The strange fossilised shells that cover the rocky foreshore at Sligo's Streedagh Point are over 300 million years old. These relics of ancient, warm-water creatures are reminders of Ireland's origins south of the equator before the continents moved and pushed northwards. An entire coral reef from that distant era lies exposed at low tide, revealing snake-like creatures that existed in a warm sea at the time of the dinosaurs.

DRUMCLIFF, CO. SLIGO

The grave of Ireland's foremost poet, WB Yeats holds an inscription chosen by the poet himself. He found inspiration in Sligo and spent his youth in the countryside, returning as a poet to stay with the Gore-Booth family of Lissadell.

ST DERBHLA'S WELL, MULLET PENINSULA, CO. MAYO

The tiny well of St Derbhla sits amid the sand dunes of

the remote Mullet Peninsula in County Mayo. She was the inspiration for a pattern day held on 1 August when people would circle the well barefoot while reciting prayers. At the end of the 'pattern', people would take three sips from the water. Calendar customs often dictated social customs; fishermen would not go to sea on Lady Day, 29 March, or on 29 September, the feast of St Michael. Bonfires were lit several times throughout the year on St John's Eve, 23 June, the feasts of Saints Peter and Paul, and at Hallowe'en, the last day of October.

CLONTUSKERT PRIORY, CO. GALWAY

The central doorway of the priory dates from the fifteenth century, and boasts a fine carving of a mermaid holding a mirror. Mermaids were carved to remind males in a religious congregation that women were the source of all lust and should be avoided. These misogynist strictures did not succeed, as many medieval Irish churchmen were married and their sons succeeded to their positions as bishops or abbots, often for several generations. It had been the tradition of Irish chieftains to donate land to the Church and then insist that a family member become the leader of the monastic community. Naturally, those given such a position wished to establish a dynasty for themselves and so they married. The son of John O'Grady, Archbishop of Cashel from 1332 to 1345, became Archbishop of Tuam, and his son, also John, became Bishop of Elphin. They were not the only ones. One of the brilliant monks who wrote the medieval Annals of Ulster had fourteen children and calmly entered their names into the margins of a manuscript as befitting the sons of a noble scribe.

THE SOUTH

The South

Over 4,000 years ago, the south of Ireland was visited by miners, most likely from Iberia, seeking precious copper ore in the rocky peninsulas of west Cork and Kerry. They were probably the people who clear-felled the primeval forests of west Cork to provide fire to split the rock and smelt the ore. They built wedge-shaped tombs in a particular style, a repeat of the tombs they left behind on the continent and brought a particular Beaker pottery that spread across the island. They were a dominant and powerful grouping for many centuries, taking timber from further and further away until the peninsulas were bare. They traded copper axes and then tin to make bronze, using the wealth to make torcs and gold necklaces of great beauty.

Wedge-shaped tomb on the Beara Peninsula

CORK CITY

The streets of Cork are usually thronged with friendly people whose lilting accent has its own melodic charm. Its shopfronts are mainly nineteenth-century, but trade here dates back to medieval times, when ships would sail right into the heart of Munster's capital, exporting hides and butter and bringing back wines and silk for the merchant princes whose fortunes built the city. Its farmland has long been a larder for Munster and its butter a staple of Ireland's diet since early times.

Unique in Ireland and the larder for a dozen restaurants and countless homes, the city's English Market holds a special place in the appetite of Cork. Exotic fruits and vegetables, and organic beef can be found alongside the

local delicacies of drisheen (sheep's blood and milk) and crubeens (pickled pigs' feet!).

ASKEATON CASTLE, CO. LIMERICK

The Banqueting Hall of Askeaton Castle (overleaf) was built by the seventh Earl of Desmond around 1440 and used for entertaining the Gaelic and Anglo-Irish nobility of Limerick in medieval times. It is surrounded by a battlemented wall and the River Deel. It was the principal seat of the FitzGeralds of Desmond and remained in the family until their defeat in the rebellions of 1579 and 1581, when their lands were confiscated and planted.

THE PUCK FAIR, KILLORGLIN, CO. KERRY

The goat is often seen as a symbol of fertility or nature and a large Billy (male) is brought down from the mountains and crowned 'king' every year in the Puck Fair Festival in Killorglin, County Kerry, an August bacchanalia of drink and music.

INCH STRAND, CO. KERRY

The vast stretch of Inch Beach, County Kerry is like some interface between nature and humankind. In winter the combination of sea, sky and wind seem to cleanse the mind and revitalise the spirit. It has provided open-air therapy for generations.

COPPINGER'S COURT, CO. CORK

Set amongst the magnificent scenery of West Cork, between Rosscarbery and Skibbereen, is the mansion of Walter Coppinger, a wealthy seventeenth-century Cork merchant. His family provided lord mayors of Cork for generations and were part of a group of families that dominated the business life of Munster. According to legend it was burnt by a servant who acted on misunderstood instructions.

BALLINACARRIGA CASTLE, CO. CORK

The Sheila-na-Gig of Ballinacarriga castle in County Cork probably dates to the early medieval period. Sheilas are curious carvings, both attracting and repelling at the same time. They would appear to be pagan and Christian, carnal and chaste, as if to remind people that pleasure and punishment were related. In general, they are found on castles and churches, and tradition suggests that they were talismans to ward off the evil eye.

SLEA HEAD, CO. KERRY

Ireland has over 3,000 kilometres of coastline from the sandy beaches of Portrush in Antrim to the slate cliffs of Slea Head. This tip of County Kerry seems the very edge of the world, facing the Blasket Islands and the endless rolling horizon of the Atlantic. Slate reefs surround the headland, ready to slice an unwary ship to pieces. It was here, in the stormy autumn of 1588 that the Santa Maria de La Rosa, one of the galleons of the ill-fated Spanish Armada anchored to re-fit and find food and water. She was caught by a rip tide that surged between the Blaskets and Slea Head. Her anchors were weak and the ship was pulled backwards onto a reef of slate just below the water line. The ship sank in under two minutes with the loss of all crew except two.

DINGLE, CO. KERRY

Dingle is one of most colourful towns in Ireland and contains some of the best restaurants and pubs anywhere. Its shopfronts display a rainbow of colour that defies any grey sky. Its seafood is the best in the country and its people some of the most charming.

THE EAST

The East

The eastern part of Ireland extending from the coastal plain along the Irish Sea to the river Shannon is known as the province of Leinster, from the Norse Viking word *'staidir'* or place and the old-Irish *'laighen'*, a name of legendary significance. According to an ancient story, a prince murdered his father and brother to become king, but left the murdered brother's child alive. The young man escaped to become a mercenary in the Roman Army, returning years later with a group of experienced soldiers. He killed the usurper and took the crown. As a reward, he granted his companions, known as *'laighen'* – Gaelic for 'spearman' – land in the east of Ireland.

BOYNE VALLEY, CO. MEATH

The river Boyne swerves through Meath in a broad curve and was the scene of perhaps the most famous battle in Irish history, the 1690 'Battle of the Boyne' commemorated on 12 July every year. It was at this point, the bend at Oldbridge, while king William was watching the Catholic army of James that a cannonball grazed his shoulder. His refusal to leave the field inspired his troops and he sent the Dutch Dragoons, the 'Special Forces' of the seventeenth century, into the river against Sir Neil O'Neill's foot regiment. In the ferocious firefight O'Neill was mortally wounded and within hours ten thousand of William's men had crossed the river. The Irish fought well and bravely, their cavalry charging again and again until casualties forced their retreat. The Battle of the Boyne established the Protestant Ascendancy that would last until Catholic Emancipation and the Land Acts of the nineteenth century.

HILL OF TARA, CO. MEATH

This extensive site has held a place in the Irish imagination for millennia. It was where priest-kings conducted elaborate ceremonies prior to Christianity and has continued to be important to pagan belief today. The oldest part of this enigmatic site was probably the focus of the ritual activity almost 4,000 years ago when early Bronze Age royalty gathered for the burial of someone they respected. The Mound of the Hostages became the tomb of a young princess who was buried with a necklace of semi-precious stones, possibly from Egypt. Her burial mound is aligned between a sacred well, 'The Well of the White Cow', and a nearby short stretch of parallel earthworks that may have been a sacred avenue to the summit and the tomb. The Hill of Tara was the source of many legends and chariot roads radiating across Ireland began on its slopes. An upright stone, the *Lia Fáil* or Stone of Destiny, was the centre of early kingship and ritual, when contenders for the throne had to circle their chariots at speed around the stone until their hubs screeched against its granite base. Another stone in the nearby churchyard has a figure, which may be Cernunnos, the god of the Celts. The site is best visited in the early morning of late evening, when slanting light throws into relief the mounds and earthworks of this once-important royal site.

THE HIGH CROSSES

The high crosses of Ireland form a corpus of art unique in western Europe. They are perhaps the most striking and original 'objects' in the Irish countryside and their shape and outline illustrate the skill and diversity of Irish stone carving. Unlike Europe and England, the crosses of Ireland have largely survived the depredations of time and are a unique testament to the Church as a patron of the arts. Many are over a thousand years old and the earliest designs suggest copies of wooden and bronze shrines: carved stone bosses and rope work around the edging and flat surfaces. They cover a wide range of subjects, principally arranged around the figure of Christ on the cross and may originally have been painted in vivid colours. The stone top of the High Cross of Muirdeach shows what a timber church would have looked like in the early Christian centuries – with a high pitched roof and crossed gable rafters.

High crosses were the perogative of rich monasteries and the finest crosses are often found near to the extensive farmland that was the source of much of monastic wealth.

Above:
Detail from Kells High Cross, Co. Meath

Right:
High Cross, Drumcliff,
Co. Sligo

Left:
High Cross, Monasterboice,
Co. Louth

DUBLIN CITY

Ireland's long-established capital city was founded by Vikings and Irish around 988. Today, the traditional street markets of Dublin reflect the multi-ethnic community that thrives in the city. Two hundred different nationalities now share in Ireland's prosperity and Nigerian bus-drivers, Polish waiters and Chinese doctors add to Dublin's cosmopolitan mix.

Old traditions still live on

LARTEY'S
Fresh Organic Produce

The elegant spire of the 'Black Church' and the 'Shamrock' lamp-standards on Dublin's north side combine Gothic revival and Celtic revival in an autumn sunset.

among the new: now surrounded by expensive apartments, the ancient Smithfield Horse Fair is still held on the first Sunday of every month when the twenty-first century is temporarily suspended in favour of haggling and dealing amid ponies, piebalds and proud young owners. Hundreds of horses, foals, saddle-makers and horsemen mingle in a rowdy gymkhana on the cobbled city streets.

Also reminiscent of earlier times are the city's food markets. In the heart of Dublin's 'Latin Quarter', the weekly Temple Bar organic market offers the very best in vegetables, bread and cheese, all organic and produced within Ireland.

The Sugarloaf Mountain, Co. Wicklow
a favourite walking spot for generations of
Dubliners.

HOLY WELL, FORE ABBEY, CO. WESTMEATH

The rag-tree of St Fechin still holds its attraction for believers, and for generations people have attached a token of their ailment to a branch, hoping for a cure. The tree and its holy well form part of a complex of medieval buildings, churches and ancient roadways which formed part of the walled town of Fore in Westmeath. The extensive gateways, walls, barbicans and old field systems suggest that Fore was a place of importance centuries ago. At one time, the

Benedictine Monastery had hundreds of students. Now it is a series of well cared for ruins beside a quaint village.

CARNSORE POINT, CO. WEXFORD

Carnsore Point is the most south-easterly point in Ireland and has always been a liminal place, somewhere between sea and land, a place where female druids lived, close to earth and sky. Ancient peoples believed it to be inhabited by the souls of drowned sailors, whose stone-covered graves lie in the sand dunes behind the sloping beach. As the sea recedes along the shingle, there is the zen-like sound of water across stone. It is truly a magical place.

Blennerville Windmill Co. Kerry

EPILOGUE

Epilogue

In some ways, Ireland's magic is that it creates memories for everyone. Its countryside has the dolmens of the earliest peoples, the castles and abbeys of medieval times, the cottages and folk traditions of more recent centuries. Its tragedies, like the Great Famine,

have left their mark on the landscape, while its busy towns and cities are proof of the country's new prosperity and success. Its music is capable of speaking to Japanese and American alike, and its culture is understandable and easily enjoyed.

Perhaps a better definition than 'magic' is needed for what this place has and is. Perhaps what Ireland offers is a

The South Pole Inn, opened by Tom Crean, the renowned Antarctic explorer.

space, somewhere between modernity and the romantic past, somewhere that imagination may roam.

And that is what the magic of Ireland really is. Because for millennia people have come to this land, some bringing just a few animals and a desperate hope, others with the sword or the Bible. All have left their mark on the landscape and on the beliefs and customs of the people. Ireland's particular magic is that it has retained small sparks of all those who have made their home on this small island on the edge of the world.

INDEX

(all distances and locations are approximate, please check on a detailed map)

Co. Limerick

Askeaton Castle: Askeaton 47

Co. Louth

Monasterboice 59

Co. Mayo

Carrigahowley Castle: 16km NW
    Westport 37
Moyne Friary: Ballina 38
Dolmen of Ballina:
    outside Ballina 39
St Derbhla's Well:
    Mullet Peninsula 42

Co. Meath

The Boyne Valley 55
Hill of Tara 56
Kells 59

Co. Monaghan

Clones Cross, Clones town 24

Co. Sligo

Streedagh Point: 24km
    N Sligo town 42
Drumcliff Churchyard: 5km N
    Sligo town 42

Co. Tyrone

Beaghmore: 13.5km NW
    Cookstown 27

Co. Westmeath

Fore Abbey:
    5km E Castlepollard 64

Co. Wexford

Carnsore Point 65

Co. Wicklow

Sugarloaf Mountain 63